CELEBRATING
MARTIN LUTHER
KING JR. DAY

BY TRUDI STRAIN TRUEIT · ILLUSTRATED BY JOEL SNYDER

The Child's World®
childsworld.com

Published by The Child's World®
1980 Lookout Drive • Mankato, MN 56003-1705
800-599-READ • www.childsworld.com

ISBN 9781503853959 (Reinforced Library Binding)
ISBN 9781503854710 (Portable Document Format)
ISBN 9781503855090 (Online Multi-user eBook)
LCCN: 2021930087

Printed in the United States of America

ABOUT THE AUTHOR

Trudi Strain Trueit is a former
television news reporter
and anchor. She has written
dozens of books for children.
She lives in Everett, WA with
her husband, Bill, a teacher.

ABOUT THE ILLUSTRATOR

Joel Snyder is a graduate of the
Rhode Island School of Design.
He has had a long career of
illustrating magazines, books, and
other projects for children and
young adults. Joel lives in upstate
New York, where he enjoys fishing
and kayaking in the Adirondack
Mountains when he's not at his
drawing board.

CONTENTS

CHAPTER 1

An American Hero

Americans of many different races join hands. Together, they march down the street and sing. Come join the parade! It's Martin Luther King Jr. Day.

Martin Luther King Jr. was an important African American leader. He worked to make sure all U.S. citizens were treated equally.

On the third Monday in January, Americans honor Martin Luther King Jr. They remember a man whose courage helped change a nation.

This country will not be a good place for any of us to live in unless we make it a good place for *all* of us to live in.
—*President Theodore Roosevelt (1858–1919)*

Some cities hold parades on Martin Luther King Jr. Day.

CHAPTER 2

Birth of a Leader

Martin Luther King Jr. was born on January 15, 1929. His family called him M.L. for short. M.L. lived in Atlanta, Georgia, with his parents, grandparents, aunt, and older sister Christine. In 1930, M.L.'s brother Alfred was born.

Children of different races lived in M.L.'s neighborhood. They all played together. One day, M.L. and Alfred went to visit two white brothers as they had always done. But the boys said their parents wouldn't allow them to play with Black children anymore.

M.L. ran to his mother. She said that some people didn't realize that beneath the skin, everyone was the same. It was painful for M.L. to lose his friends this way. He never forgot it.

M.L. was a good musician, athlete, and student. He started college at age 15.

Growing up in Atlanta, M.L played with children of other races.

CHAPTER 3

Different Races, Different Rules

When M.L. was growing up, Black and white Americans were not treated equally. In some cities, it was against the law for Black people to go to the same places as white people. They could not attend the same schools or eat in the same restaurants. Elevators and drinking fountains had signs that read "Whites Only." This was called **segregation**.

Such treatment made M.L. angry, and rightfully so. He wondered if he should hate white people. M.L.'s father was a minister. He told his son that hatred wasn't the answer. Reverend King taught M.L. that he could love others and still stand up for what he believed.

You must be the change you wish to see in the world.
—Mahatma Gandhi (1869-1948)

M.L.'s father taught him to stand up peacefully for his beliefs.

CHAPTER 4

I Have a Dream

After college, M.L. moved to Alabama and became a minister like his father. He married Coretta Scott. They had four children.

Dr. King, as he was now called, began speaking out against segregation. He led peaceful marches for **civil rights**, or equality. He gave **speeches**, too.

Dr. King led many marches for equal rights.

Dr. King's most famous speech was called "I Have a Dream."

"I have a dream that one day this nation will rise up and live out the true meaning of its **creed**; we hold these truths to be self-evident that all men are created equal," he said. "I have a dream that my four little children will one day live in a nation where they will not be judged by the color of their skin but by the content of their **character**."

We hold these truths to be self-evident, that all men are created equal, that they are endowed by their Creator with certain unalienable Rights, that among these are Life, Liberty and the pursuit of Happiness.
—*U.S. Declaration of Independence (1776) chapter 5*

Dr. King quoted the U.S. Declaration of Independence in his famous speech.

13

Taking Action

Dr. King's leadership made a difference. In 1964, U.S. President Lyndon Johnson signed the Civil Rights Act. It made segregation against the law.

Even so, some people didn't want things to change. On April 4, 1968, Dr. King was shot and killed. He was buried in Atlanta, Georgia, next to his grandmother.

In 1983, the U.S. Congress created a national holiday to honor Dr. Martin Luther King Jr. They chose the third Monday in January so the date would fall on or near Dr. King's birthday.

I've seen the promised land. I may not get there with you. But I want you to know tonight, that we, as a people, will get to the promised land.
—Martin Luther King Jr.,
"I've Been to the Mountaintop,"
April 3, 1968
(the day before his death)

President Johnson signed the Civil Rights Act in 1964.

CHAPTER 6

Celebrating Civil Rights

Church bells ring. Choirs sing angelic **hymns**. Across the nation, people gather on Martin Luther King Jr. Day. They may watch a film of one of Dr. King's speeches. Older citizens sometimes share what it was like to live during segregation.

Some Americans take part in peaceful marches. Others volunteer in their communities. They may pick up litter, paint over graffiti, or plant trees in a park.

Martin Luther King Jr. Day is a time to remember the struggle for civil rights. It is a time to remember that every American citizen should be equal and free.

> **America will never be destroyed from the outside. If we falter and lose our freedoms, it will be because we destroyed ourselves.**
> —*President Abraham Lincoln (1809–1865)*

Some people help in their communities on Martin Luther King Jr. Day.

17

CHAPTER 7

Poetry Corner

When we allow freedom to ring, when we let it ring from every village and every hamlet, from every state and every city, we will be able to speed up that day when all of God's children, Black men and white men, Jews and Gentiles, Protestants and Catholics, will be able to join hands and sing in the words of the old Negro spiritual, *"Free at last, free at last. Thank God Almighty, we are free at last."*

—*Martin Luther King Jr., "I Have a Dream,"*
  August 28, 1963

"Injustice anywhere is a threat to justice everywhere."
—*Martin Luther King Jr.*

WE WEAR THE MASK

We wear the mask that grins and lies,
It hides our cheeks and shades our eyes, —
This debt we pay to human guile;
With torn and bleeding hearts we smile,
And mouth with myriad subtleties.
Why should the world be over-wise,
In counting all our tears and sighs?
Nay, let them only see us, while
We wear the mask.

—*Paul Lawrence Dunbar (1872–1906)*

We've come to see the power of nonviolence. We've come to see that this method is not a weak method, for it's the strong man who can stand up amid opposition, who can stand up amid violence being inflicted upon him and not retaliate with violence.
—*Martin Luther King Jr., "Detroit Speech," June 23, 1963*

We who believe in freedom cannot rest.

—*Ella Baker, (1903-1986)*

CHAPTER 8

Songs of Unity

Hymns like these were often sung during U.S. civil rights marches in the 1950s and 1960s.

WE SHALL OVERCOME

We shall overcome,
We shall overcome,
We shall overcome, some day.

Chorus:
Oh, deep in my heart,
I do believe
We shall overcome, some day.

We'll walk hand in hand,
We'll walk hand in hand,
We'll walk hand in hand, some day.
(Chorus)

We shall all be free,
We shall all be free,
We shall all be free, some day.
(Chorus)

THIS LITTLE LIGHT OF MINE

This little light of mine,
I'm gonna let it shine.
This little light of mine,
I'm gonna let it shine.
This little light of mine,
I'm gonna let it shine,
Let it shine,
Let it shine,
Let it shine.

JOINING IN THE SPIRIT OF MARTIN LUTHER KING JR. DAY

* Talk to a grandparent or senior citizen about their experiences with segregation. Discuss how the civil rights movement changed attitudes toward African Americans and other groups.

* Listen to Dr. King's "I Have a Dream" speech. Write down your dreams. What are your hopes and goals for your country? How about for yourself? What can you do to be the change you wish to see in the world?

* Make the holiday a day of service. Get your friends together. Clean up trash or plant flowers in a neighborhood park.

* Visit a local historical museum with your family to learn more about Dr. Martin Luther King Jr., his life, and the fight for American civil rights.

MAKING A MARTIN LUTHER KING JR. DAY PIN

What you need:

6 inches of black yarn

6 inches of light brown yarn

6 inches of yellow yarn

1 dark brown wooden bead

1 light brown wooden bead

1 white wooden bead

Six small wiggle eyes

2 tiny black pom-poms

1 tiny white pom-poms

Red permanent marker

1 pin-back

1 toothpick

White craft glue

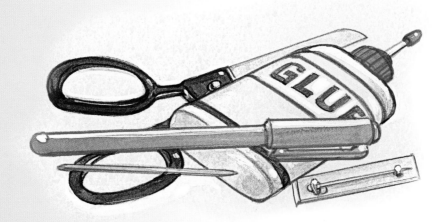

Directions

1. Cut each strip of yarn into six 1-inch pieces. (Black yarn for the dark brown bead, light brown yarn for the light brown bead, and yellow yarn for the white bead).

2. Use one end of the toothpick to dab glue inside the hole of each bead.

3. Use the other end of the toothpick to push the six ends of colored yarn into its bead.

4. Glue two wiggle eyes onto the "face" of each bead.

5. Glue a tiny pom-pom onto the bead for a nose.

6. Use the red marker to draw a mouth on each bed.

7. Glue the three beads together to make a triangle of faces.

8. Glue the pin-back to the back of the top bead.

Wear your pin proudly on Martin Luther King Jr. Day to celebrate children of all races living and playing together!

GLOSSARY

character (KAYR-ek-tur)—the quality of an individual's personality or reputation

civil rights (SIV-ull RYTS)—equality and freedom for all citizens of the United States of America

creed (KREED)—a set of beliefs

hymns (HIMZ)—songs of praise or honor

segregation (seg-reh-GAY-shun)—forcing different racial groups to be apart from one another

speeches (SPEE-chez)—talks given to audiences

LEARN MORE

BOOKS

Jazynka, Kitson. *Martin Luther King, Jr.*
Washington, DC: National Geographic, 2012.

Meltzer, Brad. *I Am Martin Luther King, Jr.*
New York, NY: Dial Books for Young Readers, 2016.

Nelson, Kadir. *I Have a Dream.*
New York, NY: Schwartz & Wade Books, 2012.

Platt, Christine. *The Story of Martin Luther King Jr.*
Emeryville, CA: Rockridge Press, 2020.

Santella, Andrew. *Martin Luther King Jr.: Civil Rights Leader.* Mankato, MN: The Child's World, 2022.

WEBSITES

Visit our website for links about Martin Luther King Jr. Day
and other holidays:
childsworld.com/links

Note to Parents, Teachers, and Librarians: We routinely verify our Web links to make sure they are safe and active sites. So encourage your readers to check them out!

INDEX